Moving through a

Season

of Grief

McDougal & Associates
Servants of Christ and Stewards of the
Mysteries of God

Moving through a

Season

of
Grief

Jerry Fitch

Published by:

McDougal & Associates
18896 Greenwell Springs Road
Greenwell Springs, LA 70739

www.ThePublishedWord.com

McDougal & Associates is an organization dedicated to spreading the Gospel of the Lord Jesus Christ to as many people as possible in the shortest time possible.

ISBN: 978-1-950398-03-4

Printed in the U.S., the U.K. and Australia
For Worldwide Distribution

DEDICATION

I dedicate this book to all those who have lost a loved one, have gone through the process of healing, and then have gone on to live a successful and fruitful life. Our journey has been a difficult one, but through perseverance, we have overcome!

ACKNOWLEDGEMENTS

First, I want to acknowledge my lovely wife and soulmate, Monique. Your faithfulness to God and His ministry has been recorded in the annals of time. Your standing alongside me through the difficulties of life has made me stronger, more focused and even more determined that nothing is impossible for us! I have been enriched *with* you, encouraged *by* you and enlarged *because of* you. I love you, Babes!

I also express my deepest appreciation to Vicki White of Freedom's Way Ministries. Vicki took on the laborious task of reviewing the original manuscript and proofing the language of the text and making the needed changes. Vicki and her husband, Jerry, have been a God-send to our ministry. Their ministry changes countless lives daily in their service to the Lord, as they desire to "win Jesus."

CONTENTS

You have turned my mourning into joyful dancing. You have taken away my clothes of mourning and clothed me with joy.

Psalm 30:11, NLT

Foreword by Jachin L. Dardar, Sr.

When I think of life and the incredible struggles that come with it, I'm reminded of what Job said: *"Man that is born of a woman is of few days, and full of trouble"* (Job 4:1). It seems that you can never be too young or too old to experience loss. The key is not only coping with it, but getting through it. None of us are exempt from the subjection of our deepest feelings and emotions to the most traumatic interruption of pain, discomfort and ultimate loss. This is all, in itself, "GRIEF!"

Although often denied by some, death is a reality to all, as is the challenge of having to deal with and ultimately overcome this thing we have come to know as grief. While no one relishes the thought of having to face this issue that is so common to man, the truth is that the only way to overcome grief is to grieve.

Everyone seems to have their own way of getting through times of difficulty and agonizing despair. Some move forward in a seemingly natural, step-by-step progression, while others experience a more complex and extended version of our God-given ability to heal. But all, in time, come to the realization and acceptance that it is a process, a very necessary one.

Sometimes the most difficult aspect of the grieving process is just getting it started in a healthy and productive manner. Having a good understanding of the issues that people may be dealing with during their time of grief becomes a vital asset in our ability to relate, console and minister to the hurting in a sensitively positive and helpful way.

There are many things in life that can cause grief, the death of a loved one being at the very top of the list. This book was written in an effort to help treat the need for realizing, understanding, promoting and, by God's grace in time of need, experiencing the healthy process of "overcoming grief."

Foreword by Jachin L. Dardar, Sr.

My heart was warmed by the invitation from one of my closest friends to write a foreword for this work dealing with life's most challenging issue. I have known Dr. Jerry Fitch for literally all of my adult life, more than forty years. Because of that, I know that the subject content of this manual comes not only from lots of study, investigation and inquiry, but also from personal experience.

Out of his own intense pain and grief, Dr. Fitch has penned a path, endeavoring to lead hurting people back to a world where there is hope of healing and a sense that, although they have been dealt a devastating blow, life is becoming again a livable experience, with all things in reasonable order and proper perspective. It is my prayer that this book will be the catalyst that incites all hurting hearts to press forward (with trust in God, who is the origin of all recovery, restoration and health) toward the true healing that is rightfully theirs.

Please examine the following pages with an open heart, an objective spirit and the faith of possibility. In doing so, you will find that the God who never meant for us to experience death is the same God who walks with us every step of the way on our journey toward overcoming grief.

Compassionately submitted,
Rev. Jachin L. Dardar, Sr.
A Friend

FOREWORD BY DARRYL MARTIN

If only it had been a knife in my back twisting from left to right, or a two-thousand-degree flame burning slowly through my flesh, or, better still, a sudden fall from a towering cliff with that all-expected abrupt stop awaiting my arrival at the base. *That* I could have dealt with. *That* I would have welcomed with open arms, as opposed to the news that I had just received—the immediacy of death in the family.

This news, unlike a knife, a fire or a fall, had no end in sight. No, this was just the beginning of a process that was initiated with a gasp for breath and then moved torturously into a state promising to take years of painful unfolding of emotions, dithering feelings, endless stress and unsettling confusion to recover from.

This was that unthinkable moment, the one we have until now refused to entertain as even a possibility in our lives. Yet, in reality, death stands before us, constantly lurking as the absolute truest certainty we can know—whether we'll allow it to penetrate our humanity or not. It is final. It has been, and it will come again. We have no choice but to do what we can to walk through this in hopes of a better day. And this, I am convinced, we *can* do—if we learn the simple principles contained in this book.

This short read is a must for clergy, counselors and the commoner alike. Having served in full-time ministry for the better part of twenty-five years, I've not only had the opportunity to study a variety of approaches to dealing with grief, but have also walked through the process with numerous parishioners who have been ruthlessly and unexpectedly thrown into the jaws of great loss.

My experiences, like the author's, have shaped the approach I now take when dealing with the grieving. But, in all fairness, I must admit that I have not suffered such a great loss as the author of this writing. While we all face some degree of loss, if indeed we've lived, I dare say that few of us will face the multiplicity of relational losses as Pastor Jerry Fitch has. This fact permits his experiential wisdom to pierce the reader's heart with a sense of being understood, and this adds hope and realism to an often unbearable situation.

Wherever you are in your course of life, I encourage you to read this book with the twofold purpose of preparing yourself for what is inevitable and of gathering understanding that can be used in an effort to comfort others who face the loss of their loved ones.

God bless you and may He add peace to you in your path to recovery. This is what David sang:

Psalm 23:1-6, GW

The LORD is my shepherd. I am never in need. He makes me lie down in green pastures. He leads me beside peaceful waters.

He renews my soul. He guides me along the paths of righteousness for the sake of his name. Even though I walk through the dark valley of death, because you are with me, I fear no harm. Your rod and your staff give me courage.

You prepare a banquet for me while my enemies watch. You anoint my head with oil. My cup overflows.
Certainly, goodness and mercy will stay close to me all the days of my life, and I will remain in the LORD's house for days without end.

Pastor Darryl Martin
Senior Pastor, New Life Church
Columbia, Tennessee

INTRODUCTION

The poet Rumi[1] wrote, "The cure for the pain is the pain," and no greater truth has been written for the healing of grief. The grieving process cannot be overlooked nor skipped. Grieving *is* the process, but, thank God, it's not the destination. There is hope in Him.

This book is not intended to be a mere compilation of statistics, although I will site a few. Nor is it meant to be an intellectual accumulation of facts derived by scientific reasoning. The content of this manual is based on more than forty-six years of hands-on ministry and a world of personal experience on the subject. The deliberate focus of the book's content is to communicate to others how to cope with and conquer one of the most basic emotions we all encounter at some point in life—grief.

---

1. A 13th-century Persian poet

According to the National Vital Statistics Report, in 2016 (the most recent year on record) alone, there were 2,744,248 deaths in the United States. That's one death every 11.5 seconds. Around the planet, 1.8 deaths occur every second! That same year, 47,173 deaths occurred by suicide in the U.S. This means that every 11 minutes a suicide is carried out. These are alarming figures, but what I believe is even more alarming is the potential of a minimum of 2,744,248 people (friends, family and others left behind) who may not be ready to deal with the grief of losing someone they love. It is to this end that this material has been written.

But these writings are not just about death. They are about victory, about overcoming for a grieving soul and being able to proceed in life with courage and hope. It is my prayer that as you read the following pages, you will be strengthened and encouraged to live out your life to the fullest. Death may sting for a while, but Paul's writings to the Corinthian church enlighten us to the fact that the sting of death is overcome by God, who gives us victory through our Lord Jesus Christ.

Therefore, let us move forward together, hand in hand, across this land with all who are reading this, and let's allow healing from grief to begin.

Jerry Fitch

IT'S REALLY TRUE

You get that phone call, the visit from a distraught family member or you hear in the wind some news you're not prepared to hear nor accept. A loved one has died. Immediately, questions fill your mind. Some of them are actually needless questions, but they are questions nonetheless. Your world has been suddenly and unexpectedly turned upside down.

Now your dreams are shattered, lives are torn, and expectations are banished. Nothing will ever be the same again—literally. The holidays for the moment will seem empty and their meanings will be changed. Anniversaries and other special occasions will not be the same. Nor will they hold the same value and importance as they previously did. The job you've worked for and that has secured your future will now seem irrelevant. You, yourself, will drastically change, and your life will not hold the same expectations as you had prior to this news. The unthinkable, the unexpected, the inexplicable has happened.

> ## Nothing will ever be
> ## the same again!

You begin to analyze what has just taken place and conclude that it's not supposed to be this way. "I'm supposed to go first," you may reason. "They were too young, too full of life and had too much to offer for this to be true. It can't be. What am I going to do without _____? Why this one and not _____."

Then, even in the midst of an insurmountable denial of the happening, the reality hits you. They're gone, and they're not coming back! Suddenly, in an instant, without warning, your life has been emptied by separation. You frantically and futilely search for answers that cannot be found.

Death happens. It is possibly the most difficult of all mysteries that we encounter in life. It has a constitution all its own. It speaks devastation and despair to our souls and spirits. If these two elements become submerged within your soul and are not resolved, they can ultimately weaken your soul and spirit.

First Corinthians 15:26 tells us that the last enemy that shall be destroyed is death. Realize that death is no friend. Whether it happens unexpectedly or you know that it is coming, either way it will touch you negatively.

Death is an enemy that affects everyone. It respects no one. It changes the mindset, the thinking processes like nothing else. It devastates lives, disintegrates futures and defies human reasoning. It happens to the undeserving, and is often unexpected. In a moment, without warning, it strikes the most healthy to the most weak, the youngest to the eldest and every group in between.

Death, by its simplest definition, is "separation," and we must learn to deal with this separation issue if we are to move on. Death separates us from a loved one, and when it happens, it's like ripping apart our very being. Suddenly a precious piece of our own soul has been taken from us.

Nothing is more debilitating than the death of a loved one. Even the strongest character is significantly weakened by this experience. The blow death deals us has no equal in this life. It cripples our emotions, dulls our senses, temporarily modifies life and ensnares all our focus.

"What am I going to do?" we ask. "How do I move on from this?"

These and countless other questions fill your mind as well as insecurities you've never had to face to this point.

Your concern for others is magnified at this time. For example, "What is Nom going to do without Dad?" You subconsciously begin to think how drastically life will change with the death of this loved one. With this horrid rush of emotions and thoughts running rampant in your mind, you attempt to analyze the what's, where's and how's of this tragedy and how this will 'fit' into your life. At the very least, life has been severely interrupted.

It's Really True

That's why I have written this book, so that death, when it comes, may not deal you a fatal blow. Through Christ and the love of your family and friends, you can overcome!

❧ 2 ❧

DEALING WITH A
DEATH BY SUICIDE

I want to attempt to assist those who have been left behind due to the suicide of a loved one. All death is tragic, but this means of losing someone seems even more tragic. Many schools of thought surround this issue. It is misunderstood, and leaves in its wake more questions than can ever be answered.

Death by suicide is unlike sickness in that a victim of death due to sickness can possibly be explained. Suicide is different. Every unanswered question has been buried with the deceased, and there is no explanation available. We are left bewildered, confused and even confounded.

Dealing with a Death by Suicide

We say things like, "I just didn't see it coming," or "I surely never expected this one to take his/her own life."

The suicide rate in our nation is alarming. Every 11 minutes a suicide is committed in America. Nearly one million individuals attempt suicide every year. Although we are told that there are multiple reasons why someone might commit suicide,

> # No theologian has ever helped me with the death of a loved one!

I would rather not deal here with the causes. That was not my purpose in writing this. Instead, I want to deal with being healed of the tragic reminders of losing a loved one.

Theologians differ on issues of eternity and how to deal with this subject of death and grieving. Actually, no theologian has ever helped me during any death, nor have most theologies. I, like many others, have found my hope and healing through trusting in a God who *cannot* and *will not* fail us, especially in such a dramatic moment of our lives.

We would do well to be reminded of what the Scriptures say: The secret things belong to God (see Deuteronomy 29:29).

I know how I feel about death, but I've often wondered how those who have gone before me felt about leaving us. What I'm about to say next will help all who have lost someone to death, not only to suicide, but to *any* cause of death. I have heard it said many times over that if those who have died could return, they wouldn't do it. Have you heard that before? How does that make you feel? Personally, I have taken offense at that conclusion.

I find no comfort in thinking that, through the separation caused by death, those whom I've loved and continue to love and who have loved me would think or say that if they *could* return, they still *wouldn't* do it. To think that somehow, through a tragic separation, there was such a drastic change of heart from wanting to be with me to not wanting to be with me ... how could that be true?

The Scriptures can bring comfort to those who have lost a loved one by suicide or any other means. Paul wrote to the believers in Thessalonica:

Dealing with a Death by Suicide

But we, brethren, being taken from you for a short time in presence, not in heart, endeavoured the more abundantly to see your face with great desire.   1 Thessalonians 2:17

When Paul said that he had been taken from the Thessalonians *"in presence, not in heart,"* I believe that he was giving us insight, not only in the natural, but also concerning the life to come. Hear the heart of the one speaking: "I may not be with you, but I *want* to be with you." To me, Paul was saying, "I would come back if I could."

Life may not be perfect, but separation is not final! I am not convinced that eternal separation changes our feelings that much, except to magnify them. I want to change the statement that says, "Even if they *could* come back, they *wouldn't*." I would say it this way: "If they *could* return, they *would*, but since they can't, then it's better for us to go to them."

God has a timing for us to be reunited with our loved ones, and we are not to infringe upon that timing by taking matters into our own hands. In the meantime, we can be assured that they would want to be back with us, and that is comforting. This is where the healing begins. You have not been rejected or abandoned! Get those thoughts out of your spirit.

Luke 16 also gives us some perspective on life after death. Abraham, according to this passage, said, *"There is a great chasm separating us. No one can cross over to you from here, and no one can cross over to us from there"* (verse 26, NLT).

Your loved one would come back if he or she could!

I understand that no one wants to go to Hell, but that's not my point. My point is that when we have entered our eternal abode, we *cannot* go back. It's not that we *don't want to*; we *cannot*. Find solace in knowing that your loved one *would* come back if he or she *could*.

Here we find the answer to life's greatest difficulty, and herein is our source of strength, that as humans we may have a life of hardships—separation from our loved ones being the greatest, but Heaven is the answer! In Heaven, there are no difficulties, no sicknesses, no sorrows, no pain, no misery, no heartbreak and nothing else that denies a person the perfection of life.

In his letter to the Thessalonians, Paul added:

> *For what is our hope, or joy, or crown of rejoicing? Are not even ye in the presence of our Lord Jesus Christ at his coming?*
>
> 1 Thessalonians 2:19

Our hope, our joy and our crown of rejoicing is to be in the presence of the Lord Jesus Christ. In His presence is our perfection. Life here on earth may not be perfect, but Heaven is perfect, perfect because of the presence and the person of our Lord Jesus Christ.

Although we cannot know what a person who has committed suicide was thinking, we can have some clues to their thought processes. Take, for example, a loving, nurturing, caring wife, mother and daughter who is filled with laughter and joy and seemingly has no animosities about life and living. One moment she is enjoying her husband, children and grandchildren and the next moment she is found lifeless, having taken her own life—seemingly without rhyme or reason. Can you imagine that this person who was enjoying life to the fullest was contemplating suicide?

> # A suicide victim is just that—a victim!

Personally, I can't imagine it. And yet this has been the case with many victims of suicide who were taking some sort of medication because of depression, anxiety or any number of other emotional maladies. It is my persuasion that the suicide victim is just that—a victim.

In other words, these people didn't kill themselves. It wasn't in their nature to do this. Suicide was not part of their thought pattern, and they had no desire whatsoever to take their own lives or to leave their loved ones behind.

Dealing with a Death by Suicide

It was an outside influence that committed this heinous act. Our loved ones were not themselves when they did this. I cannot emphasize this enough.

Forget the fallacies about insanity causing it. The truth is that relatively few people with mental illness attempt suicide. Also disregard the popular opinions about suicide being the result of sadness, dissatisfaction with life in general and all the other misconceptions.

> **Their lives were stolen by the enemy of our souls!**

These people were not motivated by any rational thinking. They didn't do this. They loved you and the rest of their friends and family. They had a zest for life and were anticipating a wonderful future. They didn't take their lives; their lives were stolen by the enemy of our souls.

❧ 3 ❧

MY EXPERIENCE
WITH GRIEF

Although I am not a professional in this arena of grief, I have certainly had many occasions to minister to people who were struggling with grief, and I have also had to overcome this enemy myself. Over more than forty years of ministry, I have compiled many observances of those who grieve, and I can also tell you my personal experiences.

Some professionals will tell you that there are five stages of grief, while others adhere to seven. Regardless of what others advocate, the actual grieving process varies as much as the individuals who experience the loss of a loved one. There is not one set of rules that applies to everyone. Yet there are things that can be done by all that will usually assist in getting over grief.

Overcoming grief appears to be accomplished in stages, but these stages usually overlap and extend for varied periods of time. For example, I've noticed that at first there is much talk about all the good qualities of the departed. "He could do no wrong." "She was the best wife (or relative or neighbor) anybody could ever have hoped to have."

> **It is good to cry!**
> **It is good to laugh!**
> **It is good to do nothing at all!**

Nothing negative is mentioned. This is good. It is important to focus on the positives of the person, for that allows healing to begin. In time, conversations about the deceased will include a more complete description of their total person.

Your response to a grieving individual should coincide with the feelings they are experiencing at that moment. If you are to assist them in overcoming their grief, timing is important, and you must be sensitive to their mood. Here are some behavioral patterns I have witnessed in grieving parties, beginning with the first news of losing a loved one through to the ultimate acceptance and healing of the person.

Denial, shock and blame are usually the first emotions to arise and overtake the person left behind.

Then, in time, anger sets in. It doesn't seem fair that the loved one has departed.

Loneliness usually follows the burial ceremony and lingers for an indefinite period of time.

Reminiscing over the departed loved one is good as it allows emotions—both good and bad—to be expressed. Suppressed emotions are very unhealthy and tend to bring more unnecessary hardship upon you as you seek to overcome grief.

It is important to say this: it's good to cry, it's good to laugh, and it's also good to do nothing at all. In other words, do what you feel you need to do, and don't suppress your emotions. Realize that this is not a systematic regimen that has to go by the numbers. Any one or all of the above emotions will occur during your journey to healing from grief. Don't be afraid to admit and face them openly.

My Experience with Grief

There will come a time when your loss will no longer hurt. It will no longer cause you pain. Also, that loss will no longer be off limits to speak about. That may seem impossible right now, but I assure you that day will come.

The acceptance of a person's death does not mean that you no longer remember them. It means that you have finally been healed of the hurt of losing them. It may take years to fully reach this place, but it doesn't take years to begin the journey of getting over your loss.

In my own personal experience, death took my baby sister Sheila (she was my baby sister at the time; I now have a few other baby sisters). Death also took my mother, my father, a brother and a son. With each of these deaths, the grieving process differed.

I was relatively young, only seven, when my baby sister Sheila passed away from sickness. She was only thirty days old. My hurt came mostly from observing the hurt my parents were experiencing.

Then, Mamma passed away from blood clots on her lungs when I was twenty-five and she was just forty-four. You can imagine how hard that was on all of us. As the oldest boy in the family, I had been taught that I had to be strong for the sake of others. This assigned role did not allow me to grieve publicly. This was terribly wrong. It is not an uncommon concept, but it comes from an insensitive line of reasoning, and it does great damage to the soul of the individual.

To my determinant, I thought I had to soldier on and I went back into the pulpit too soon after Mama's passing, the Sunday following her burial. The result was that I struggled for a time as a preacher, a pastor, a husband and a father. My teaching (or lack of teaching) in this area had harmed me.

I finally went through the process of grieving, but only after much harm had been done to those I loved and to myself. I loved my mom and I still do. I missed her terribly, and I still do. Now, however, I don't think about her as frequently as I did in the past, and it's hard for me to remember the sound of her voice. That voice stayed with me for many years.

When Daddy died, twenty-six years later, I was presented with a very different process of grieving than with either my sister or mother. I had loved and respected my father my whole life. Now, with his passing, I was suddenly overcome with anger. I was angry with him and angry with myself. (I'll deal with this issue more in detail in a later portion of the book). I remember what Daddy's voice sounded like in the latter part of his life. It was coarse because of a stroke he had suffered. I also remember the sound of his voice in correction during my earlier years and his mannerisms, the way he let us know, in no uncertain terms, that he meant business and we'd better heed him.

> # Pain, denial and unbelief filled the room!

In 2011, I also lost my dear brother Wesley. Wesley was much more than a brother. He was a close friend and a fellow minister. The grieving process I went through with his passing was, again, different, and it was difficult.

Before Wesley died, he and I spoke on the phone every day. Then my wife and I actually moved in with him and his dear wife, Brenda, to assist in the process of caring for him. I was able to gain much understanding of the dying process as I watched a young man who loved life and loved people slowly give way to the grip of death. I still recall vividly much of the sequence of his passing. Pain, denial and unbelief filled the room as we watched him breathe his last, and we all responded differently to that moment.

It has now been eight years since Wesley was taken from us. The pain is still fresh, the memories are cherished, and the questions still persist, perhaps not as much as they did earlier.

As much as I miss Shelia, Momma, Daddy and Wesley, none of their deaths could compare to the hurt I experienced when my son, Bubba, was taken later in 2011. If there is such a thing as extreme emotions in each stage, I believe I reached them all with Bubba's passing. I was not only affected emotionally and mentally, but physically as well. I have never hurt so much from anything as from the loss of my beloved son.

It took at least two years for me to overcome the grief of losing Bubba. Do I still hurt? Yes, I do. Do I still miss him? Yes, I do. Is his memory still fresh after eight years? Yes, it is. But it's different now.

My Experience with Grief

It's no wonder that, in the resurrection of Jesus from the dead, He first dealt with the most difficult emotion of all—grief! In the resurrection, He conquered grief so that we can conquer it as well, with His help.

☙ 4 ❧

WHAT CAN YOU DO?

It is important for the grieving to surround themselves with loved ones. Whatever you do, don't try to do this by yourself. If at all possible, avoid being alone.

Following a funeral service, families often accompany a grieving person to their home. Typically they stay for a few hours, but then, one by one, they excuse themselves and leave the grieving person behind, alone. This is so wrong! If you really want to help someone overcome grief, make yourself available to stay with them as long as they need you. Understand that they are now facing one of the worst feelings anyone can have—severe loneliness. This loneliness is a terrible thing. To surround them at the most horrifying time of their lives and then abandon them only compounds their loneliness.

The next thing to understand is that there may not be that much need for you to talk. The grieving person will want to talk, so let them do the talking, and you do the listening. Become an ear, not a counselor. You will have ample opportunity to speak into their lives, and when you do, you must be careful what you say.

> **The best thing to do is to be there, be available, and say as little as possible!**

Any immediate conversations with the grieving party should be initiated by *them*. The best thing to do is to be there, be available and say as little as possible. Although it may be difficult to decipher when to talk and when to hold your peace, use common sense and guard your words.

Please be careful what you say to a grieving person. For example, do *not* say, "I know how you feel." You probably don't unless you've lost the same loved one. Another thing not to say is this, "I know what you're going through." You probably don't. Another phrase to avoid is, "You'll get over it." Can you understand how very insensitive that is? Perhaps one of the worst things to say is, "They're in at a better place." For the grieving one left behind, this doesn't ring true. Don't assume to know everything at this moment.

Be sensitive, flexible and loving in your willingness to console a grieving friend or loved one. I would add that in most of my experiences with grieving people, very few of their friends have said words that actually encouraged them. Sadly, most ministers parrot what they've been taught. But it's not always comforting to hear that my loved one is in a better place. I'm sure we all mean well by by saying this, but please heed the advice of one who's been on both sides of this issue. When you don't know what to say, it's better to say nothing at all. Just be there to love the grieving person and listen to them.

⊱ 5 ⊰

DEALING WITH EMOTIONS

We are created by God, and in His omniscient ways, He has made us emotional beings. Our God is a God of emotions. I read in His Word that He laughs, weeps and grieves. Therefore, it is incumbent upon us to learn about these emotions and how to respond to them properly.

> ## The first step is usually the most difficult!

The purpose of this writing is not so much to define in depth these emotions but, rather, to discover how they relate to grief and how to be healed from them when faced with the reality of death.

Upon receiving the news of the death of a loved one, there seems to be an immediate uprising of denial, certain shock and blame.

"No! I can't believe it! It's not true!"

"Who did this?"

"Why did this happen?"

"How did it happen?"

It somehow seems that if I can block out the reality of death through denial, it will just go away, like a bad dream.

"I don't want this to be true! It can't be true!"

"Who? Why? Where?"

These are all natural responses to death. Although denial does not change the fact, it is the beginning stage of healing.

Denial is an automatic response to the distress one is sensing and actually is the catalyst that initiates the process. If an emotion is not expressed, then healing cannot begin. As difficult as it may seem at the moment, denial, as well as the other emotions which follow, are good and beneficial to healing. It is like starting on a long journey. The first step is usually the most difficult, but unless that step is taken, the destination can never be reached.

Denial is more than just saying, "I don't believe it happened." It is a disowning of what has happened. This is a temporary coping mechanism which allows you to deal with the moment reality of it finally takes hold. The initial emotion, as difficult as it may be, opens the door for healing to begin.

> # Many who suppress anger become bitter!

Anger and bitterness eventually arise as emotions that compound the pain of not understanding why death has occurred. It may be anger at the deceased one, anger at yourself or even anger at God for allowing this to happen. Many who suppress anger become bitter, and soon the character of the grieving one changes.

In actuality, they take on a new identity, one that is not their own. The danger is that depression may result from this suppression. Please understand that

I'm not advocating that you vent your anger by taking it out on someone nearby. The expression of anger I'm speaking about does not lash out at others. Rather, it expresses a feeling that may not be understood at the time but is released within. This is a feeling of helplessness, not being able to change the circumstances of the event.

Loneliness is possibly the only emotion that must be dealt with by the person alone. Please understand. I'm not saying that the grieving one is to be left alone. Actually, just the opposite should be done, as I noted earlier. If you are to assist this person in the healing process, stay with them for a while.

> **Loneliness must be dealt with by the person alone!**

Often a grieving person will say they don't want company, don't want anyone around. Sometimes they are telling the truth (although the idea is not very healthy in my opinion). At other times they may just be saying that. I must emphasize: a grieving person needs to be surrounded by loving, happy, caring and understanding family and friends.

Have you ever heard the expression, "lonely in a crowd?" Loneliness is not a lack of people in your life; loneliness is emptiness within that cannot be filled with friends or family. With the death of a loved one, there comes a loneliness, a void that seemingly can never be filled. The relationship of the departed one to the grieving party will determine how deep the hurt is and also how to recover from the loss. Even though that void seemingly cannot be filled, you can be healed of this hurt.

I know, so please allow me to share a personal experience here. No one can ever take the place of my son. I have two other sons, but they have their own place in my life. I do miss Bubba, but after eight years of separation from him, I can say that it's okay now. Do I still have times when **I** want to weep? Yes, I do. Do I still miss him? Yes, I do. Each time I look at a photo he is in, memories return, but now I enjoy the good times I had with him.

Do I still hurt? Yes, I do, but only occasionally. And now the hurt is no longer the devastating kind of hurt; it's more like a brief recall of the pain I suffered, without the actual suffering. It's amazing how God has brought healing to my being without removing the memories that I cherish of my son. The old saying, "Time heals all wounds," is absolutely correct.

> # In acceptance, we are healed!

Acceptance is our destination, for in acceptance we are healed. Some may feel that if they accept what has happened, they have forsaken the deceased loved one. Actually the opposite is true. In acceptance, it is not a forsaking that takes place but, rather, a returning.

What do I mean by that? I mean that I can finally enjoy the life I once had with the departed one although they are no longer here to enjoy it with me. I am "normal" again; life is good and fulfilling again. Yes, one day I want to be reunited with my loved ones who have gone on before me. But for now, I want to live life to the fullest. I am no longer dealing with the guilt associated with the passing of my loved one or the process of being healed of the resulting emotions. Everything is back into perspective, and I can move on.

ぺ **6** ಬ

THE DANGER OF
PUTTING OFF GRIEF

There have been instances where people have "put off" grieving for some time, but when a person does this, it is only for a moment. Grief may seem to be safely buried in your psyche, but it will raise its ugly head one day and continue to do so until it is once and for all faced and successfully dealt with.

Although I have only witnessed this occurrence a few times in my ministry, it does happen. An individual may try to "lose" themselves by becoming involved in doing "stuff." While getting involved in activities is a good thing (it can assist a person in healing from grief), to totally disregard grieving by becoming active is simply postponing the inevitable.

The Danger of Putting Off Grief

Please understand that this individual loved the departed one deeply. In fact, it is possible that their love was so deep that this person may have unconsciously continued denying the death of the loved one. The absence of the departed caused them sorrow, but their sense of missing them somehow seems temporary. This prevents the individual from grieving and accepting the reality that the loved one will not return—ever.

> **Actual Healing begins when the reality of death is accepted!**

What happens when a person puts off true grieving is that a certain form of grief is taking place, but the actuality of grieving is missing. Some may say that this sort of grieving is best, for it may lessen the impact over time. Frankly, I believe the opposite is true. When this happens, the grieving process is just dragged out over time, but it ultimately overtakes the individual. Actual healing begins when the reality of death is accepted.

Some characteristics of those who put off grief are:

1. Total denial within, while verbally acknowledging the passing of the loved one.
2. The false anticipation that the departed one will renter their lives.
3. Mood swings: positive emotions while engaged in some activity and then negative emotions when the activity is complete. Some unconsciously assume a new identity, abandoning who they are and living out who they become because of not being healed.
4. A sense of "not being able to get over" the death of the loved one.
5. A sense of being consumed (emotionally and mentally) with the death of the loved one.

The expected end of the person who puts off grief:
1. A total nervous breakdown.
2. A future filled with emptiness and pain, never experiencing healing—emotionally and mentally.
3. At the very worst, an untimely death.
4. The inability to enjoy healthy relationships.

(They cannot love another because of always comparing others to the deceased person).

I compare this individual with a functional alcoholic. This kind of alcoholic can seemingly function as a normal person, performing every activity expected of him on a daily basis, and yet denying the fact that he or she is an alcoholic. When the day is over and the crowds are gone, they are faced with the truth that alcoholism is consuming their total being. Still, they deny that they are an alcoholic.

> **Any individual who refuses to acknowledge their avoidance of grief will ultimately be devastated!**

Devastation, for this individual, is as close as their alcoholism being discovered. Eventually they can no longer hide and must deal with the fact or plunge headlong into the destruction awaiting them.

Any individual who refuses to acknowledge their avoidance of grief will ultimately be devastated, but it will not come from others discovering their avoidance grief. It will occur when the finally realize that they have not grieved, only hidden the facts by talking about their hurts, while still wondering "why can't I get over this?" This individual may function in an inebriated state of disguised grief and actually seem normal, even fully functional. The truth is that deep within this person is longing for the freedom to truly be normal again.

"When will it stop hurting?"

"Why can't I get over this pain?"

"Why did you leave me?"

These are questions that we all ask in grief, but there must come a time when we settle these question within ourselves and move on. The key to getting over the grief of losing a loved one is simply to grieve and then move on.

No, it's not easy, but it's a choice that we must make in order to heal. We must all do this, or we will ride the roller-coaster of grief until it crashes upon us and brings a devastation into our lives that is much more serious than the death of the loved one itself.

Here are some things that can help:

- Acknowledge "Something is wrong with me."
- Stop trying to convince yourself that you have already grieved.
- Release the flood of emotions associated with grief.
- Acknowledge that your loved one is never returning, but, in God's timing, you will go to be reunited with him or her.
- Talk to someone who really can help you. I say "really" because not everyone can. Others empathizing and sympathizing with you after a long and extended period of grief is not helping. Instead, it actually feeds the dilemma you're in.
- Move on and begin the healing process so that you can actually relate to the loss of the loved one without being devastated within.
- Finally, look to tomorrow; that's where your true hope lies.

☙ 7 ❧

WHEN YOU ARE FOREWARNED

To this point, we have discussed the subject of grief in conjunction with someone who has passed away suddenly and unexpectedly. Handling the grief and overcoming it takes more than a systematic set of rules that one follows. We have examined some of the emotions and the moods one experiences during this difficult time and suggested ways to overcome the hurts and return to living a life without the hindrances of grief holding us back. We have learned that we can and will return to normal and can lead a successful life without the pain hindering us following the traumatic loss of a loved one. But what about when you know that a friend or loved one has a limited time left to live? How do you deal with that grief? When does the grieving begin? And how does it affect you?

I want to say again that there is not a 1-, 2-, 3-step program to follow. As with all grieving, each individual will deal differently when receiving the news that a loved one or a friend has only a certain amount of time left to live. Whether it's one month or one year, that news will hit you with a devastation that needs to be dealt with. Subsequent emotions will arise, then subside, then arise again.

Unbelief seems to be the first of the many emotions that will surface, followed by fear and loneliness and, quite possibly, anger that will cause you to "take a stand" against the news of the impending death of your loved one. The emptiness that is experienced is beyond reality, even while your loved one is still around.

Let's start by answering these questions: "How do you deal with the grief once you know that a loved one has a limited time to live? When does the grieving begin? And how does it affect you?" As I said earlier in the book, I will be speaking from many years of pastoral experience dealing with those who have lost loved ones, as well as from my own personal losses. It appears to me that grieving begins when we come to realize it is inevitable that death will occur unless a miracle of some kind happens. The grieving cannot begin until we come to acknowledge that fact. Therefore, timing becomes an issue. Even if you "don't give up," once you've made a mental assessment and have accepted the fact that death is imminent, grieving begins.

> **In the deepest recesses of your being, something tells you their time is limited!**

I know that this last statement may seem contradictory, but it isn't. So many of us fight this bitter battle until the very end and even beyond (I'll explain what I mean by this later). We look death squarely in the face, defying its very right to be there, trusting and believing God for the miracle, yet, at the same time, acknowledging that unless a turnaround takes place, we will soon lose our loved one.

It is here, at this point, that grieving begins. You may have a resolve within you that says, "It's not going to happen; I'll do whatever it takes; I'll never give up," and you may really mean everything you're saying. But somehow, in the deepest recesses of your being, something tells you this person's time is limited. Then the grieving begins. It's not that you're giving up; it's the realization of the inevitable that causes grief to take hold.

Now, let me explain what I meant when I said, "Many of us fight this bitter battle until the very end and even beyond." When I first heard the news about my brother Wesley having a tumor in his colon, I was hurt. He was my little brother, and as his big brother, I felt that I should be able to take care of the situation. Surgery was performed, the tumor was removed, and treatment began.

When I heard about the treatment, I realized that the situation was more serious than I had been led to believe. Those who have been through this understand the roller coaster of emotions that I went through at this point. It seemed as if every emotion

I have ever sensed flooded my mind at once, leaving me with more questions than answers.

What did the doctors mean when they said, "First, chemo, then, possibly, radiation, and if that doesn't work, then other alternative treatments?" I was rejecting the possibility of my younger brother dying, and I continued to reject it until the very end!

Then one day Wesley called me. He asked me if Monique and I would be willing to come and move in with him and Brenda and help her take care of him. Without hesitation, we resigned the church we were pastoring in Jacksonville, Florida, and moved in with Wesley and Brenda in Dulac, Louisiana, to assist them during this most difficult time of their lives.

Wesley passed away on a Wednesday. Earlier in the day, he was in and out of consciousness, but I told him that I was still believing God for a miracle. We had spoken about it a number of times before, and he agreed with me. "J," he said, (my close friends and family members called me that), "I don't want to die, but I'm ready if I have to. BUT I'm believing God for a miracle. You believe with me."

He had never believed for anything else, and neither did I. And why should we believe for anything else? We had seen God intervene so many times in the past that we refused to believe for anything less than a miracle. We had seen God heal incurable diseases. We had even seen Him raise people up from their death beds.

God had healed us before. He healed Wes when, as a young boy, doctors couldn't figure out why he was losing so much weight and becoming lifeless. God had intervened then, and He could surely do it again.

> **I'm believing God for a miracle. You believe with me!**

I reassured Wes that I would not give up and would continue praying for a miracle. As I watched life leaving his body that very evening, I continued to pray for a miracle. Four hours later, when the coroner arrived, I was still praying for a miracle. Even as I assisted the men in loading Wes into the hearse in the wee hours of the morning, I breathed my last prayer for a miracle as they drove away. That is what I meant when I said "until the end and beyond."

The time period from Wesley's surgery to the moment he went on to his eternal reward was approximately a year. I can assure you that the grieving process began long before Wesley died. So many of the emotions we experienced during his actual death had been reconciled long before.

Did we eventually give up? Never, absolutely not! Did we experience emotional ups and downs? Oh, yes, every day. Did the process of overcoming the pain continue following Wesley's death? Yes, it did, and it continues today. But we are closer to victory over these emotions today than we were a year ago.

If you're currently in a position where you are caring for a loved one or friend, or if you've received the news that your friend or family member has a limited time to live, let me encourage you to stand strong. But whatever emotion you are presently facing, embrace it. Don't deny it or squelch it. This will allow healing to begin.

When You Are Forewarned

Move positively about in your daily routine, continuing to believe for a turnaround, and continue being the encourager you were meant to be. And know this: you're going to make it, and you're going to make it in fine fashion.

ॐ **8** ॐ

ARE YOU WORTHY OF
ABSOLUTE TRUST?

Absolute defined means "used to give strong emphasis to what is being said, having total power and authority, not capable of being viewed as partial or relative, not depending on or qualified by anything else, complete and in no way conditional on any future evidence or behavior." [2]

Trust defined means "confidence in and reliance on good qualities, especially fairness, truth, honor or ability. Hopeful reliance on what will happen in the future. Responsibility for taking good care of somebody or something."[2]

It would be difficult to understand how any person could be totally impartial in every circumstance.

2. Encarta Dictionary

In fact, very few people can actually say that given any situation, they *could* be, much less *would* be, impartial in that circumstance.

Trust is a learned behavior. The more you prove that what you say you're going to do, you actually do, the more trust you earn. We have all heard it said, "Trust is not given; it's earned." It seems to be true, doesn't it?

I get somewhat tickled by the trickery of television commercials when merchandising their products. They hire a paid spokesperson to promote their product, and often you'll hear that spokesperson (perhaps a known personality) say, "Trust me, I know!" But how can you trust someone you don't know? Trust is relational. It comes by knowing someone and observing their behavior, not by a paid spokesperson used to manipulate you.

> **Can my dying friend or family member have absolute trust in me?**

But put these two words together—ABSOLUTE TRUST—and you have someone everyone would be jealous of. "Absolute trust?" Is it possible that a person can have that kind of confidence in another individual? Are you a person of absolute trust? I cannot answer that question for you or for anyone else. Only you can answer it.

> **They are looking to you for help, believing you will not violate their trust!**

I know I have absolute trust in God, but is it possible to have absolute trust in another person? Have you ever trusted a person, only to have that trust violated? That hurts, and it adversely affects the possibility of ever trusting others. But the real question at hand in regard to overcoming grief is this, "Can my dying friend or family member have absolute trust in me?" Now, that's a different story isn't it?

When a loved one's prognosis is negative, much of what is in their heart, as well as ours, surfaces. In this grievous time, there is the very real possibility that you will be asked to do things you normally would not be asked to do. Your dying loved one is asking for absolute trust from you. They are looking to you for help, believing that you will not violate what they have entrusted to you (whatever their final requests). Your trustworthiness becomes very important to them. Can they depend on you that you will honor exactly what you say you'll do?

Those who are or have been in the position of caring for a loved one who has been given little time to live will understand what I'm saying here. I have found, through experience, that honesty is the best policy. Be as honest as you can in your responses. Some might say, "Well, it won't be long, and they'll be gone, and it won't matter then." It may be true they will be gone shortly, and then it won't matter *to them*, but it will still matter *to you*.

Very often a person who is dying is looking for security that their loved ones will be cared for and that some pending business will be handled properly. They may make a request for you to handle this unfinished business. Comfort them, but carefully answer their requests.

My brother asked me to care for his wife Brenda once he was gone. Although he still did not believe he would die, he loved his wife and wanted to be sure that she would be taken care of. My response (which seemed to satisfy him) was simply that Monique and I would take care of her as much as she would allow us to.

> **We are, at times, tormented by the feeling that we didn't do enough!**

He asked me to believe with him for a miracle and, as I stated in the last chapter, I believed until the end and beyond. He seemed to trust me completely, and I refused to violate that trust. What I couldn't do I told him, and what I could do I did. This helped me to receive healing and overcome the grief I felt. I was so glad that I had not violated the trust my brother had placed in me.

One of the most serious hurdles to overcoming grief (and one that many deal with) is a guilty conscience. We are, at times, tormented by the feeling that we didn't do enough or that we could have done something differently. Whatever you do, refuse to live with a guilty conscience. As difficult as it seems, I believe it is better to be honest than to have to deal with our dishonesty later. There is always guilt that accompanies dishonesty, and that may be even harder to overcome.

Please understand: I'm not saying that you *cannot* or *will not* overcome the guilt that comes with dishonesty. I'm saying that it's best not to add to all the emotional drama you will surely face. with the death of a loved one With God's help, we can overcome any and every emotion.

Another area of guilt that some deal with is questioning, "Why did this one go, when it *should* have been me." I don't know if you've ever felt this way or known someone who has, but it's a very real sense of guilt that haunts many.

Often this feeling springs from another source, other than the death of a loved one. When my son passed away, one of his uncles wept at his casket and asked me, "Why did he have to go? Why didn't God take me instead?" He demonstrated one of the truest senses of guilt that I have ever witnessed. He actually felt that my son should have lived and he should have died. Regardless of the origin of this guilt, it's a very real emotion and must be dealt with in order to overcome grief.

> ## Do not allow a guilt-ridden conscience to destroy you!

How a person deals with this guilt varies as much as those who experience it. Some may plunge headlong into trying to eliminate their pain through sedatives, some through alcohol. Others choose to live with it for the rest of their lives.

If you or someone you know is going through this, let me says: You were left here for a purpose. I may not be able to define that purpose, but I can say what that purpose is *not*. It is not so that you will waste the remainder of your life crippled by the effects of guilt. You are not responsible for the fact that some other person has died before you, and whether you ever understand why it happened to them and not to you is not relevant.

Are You Worthy of Absolute Trust?

This is not your fault. Therefore, do not let a guilt-laden conscience destroy you over something you had no control over. Rather, begin to understand that this feeling of guilt is unfounded. You had no control over their death, so refuse to succumb to the grip of guilt in your life.

Instead, realign your focus on what you should be doing next. Embrace life and live it to the fullest!

If the guilt persists, I would suggest that you review the final chapter entitled "Closing Remarks." It will assist you to overcome and conquer the remaining guilt and grief you may still be sensing.

Here are some observations that should help you with these issues:

1. Love your dying loved one enough to be truthful yet hopeful.
2. Your loved one trusts you. Don't violate that trust.
3. Living with a clear conscience is better than dying with a guilty one.
4. Speak what's really in your heart before it's too late.

5. I've learned that you can have absolute trust in a person.
6. More importantly, I've learned that a person can have absolute trust in me.
7. Develop a lifetime of qualities that will endear you to others.
8. Since God has put you in someone's life, He trusts you to do and say what is right.
9. Always remember, "I can do this. I can and will overcome grief!"

Without a doubt, a prolonged sickness can take its toll on family members and friends. It may not be about us, but following the passing of a loved one, we are left behind to pick up the pieces and try to make some sense of it all.

A note of caution would do well here: Be careful what you say and how you handle certain situations with friends and family members during this time. The stress and hurt you may be experiencing could cause you to inadvertently say or express something that you may not otherwise have said at any other time. You surely do not want to add to already hurt feelings by allowing stress to take control of your thoughts and actions.

Are You Worthy of Absolute Trust?

This brings me to a very important point: do not wear yourself out. Find times for rest and relaxation. Some may say, "I'm not here to rest; I'm here to help," and that's true. But a person who is mentally stressed and physically worn out cannot provide the help a well-rested person can. Your loved ones need you, so you need to be able to give them your very best.

ଓ 9 ଅ

DEALING WITH MEMORIES

In this chapter, we will discuss the effects that memories have upon us. Memories affect us in many ways—some positive and some negative. But make no mistake about it, memories will show up and make an impact on our lives.

> **What you will make, from this moment on, are memories!**

Memories are the eyes of our yesterdays. They have a way of taking us back to a far distant past and also of bringing us as close as today. All that you have of your last moment and the rest of your past are memories. What you will make, from this moment on, are memories.

Memories can be triggered many ways, such as through conversation, through looking at photos or simply just thinking back on an event or a person. Memories can show up even without thoughts, conversation or any other outside stimulus. To be truthful, all you can take into today and tomorrow from yesterday are memories.

Memory is an amazing faculty that God has created within us. Although some memories are painful, I believe that there are healing virtues within them, put there by God Himself.

The earliest memory I have is as a child, standing beside Daddy's car in my underwear. When I recounted this event to Momma, I asked her how old she thought I was. To her amazement (and mine), she said I couldn't have been more than two.

Why would this memory stay with me while so many other significant ones seemed to disappear? I seem to remember so many events of my early childhood (before I attended school), and yet most seem to have little or no relevance to me.

I remember being a happy child)except when I got a whipping, and that seemed to happen often). I did chores, walked everywhere barefooted, had little to wear, ran around the plantation like a wild Indian. (Before some get offended at this, I am 100% American Indian). I played, I had dogs (King and Queen), cats, chickens and a pet alligator that stayed with me in my room, as well as other farm animals.

> **All you can take into today and tomorrow from yesterday are memories!**

I ran in the sugar cane fields, swam in the bayou, ate the food provided for us, worked in the garden, baled hay, operated the tractor in the cane field and went to the outhouse. I somehow didn't realize that the dark-skinned people who lived on the plantation were of a different race. I ate and slept with them and got whippings from them when I was bad. I bathed in a #3 tub (when we bathed, that is). I brought snakes into the house. Daddy made me put them outside, and then he'd whip me. After all, they were water moccasins.

I loved to play in the rain during lightning storms (I didn't say I was smart), and Mom and Dad didn't even seem to mind. I had a crush on the neighbor's daughter (her name was Marylyn), and so forth and so on ... All this before I began attending school. It was, you know, just a normal childhood.

These memories and so many others (such as from my adolescence, my teen years and all the period growing up into adulthood) are etched into my mind, and they often "visit" me at a moment's notice. Some of them are positive. For instance, I remember when I preached my first message, gave my first altar call, received my first offering and officiated my first funeral. I remember the joy of having my first child (and then the joy of the three others). Others are negative. For instance, the hurts I suffered in my years of ministry—the opposition to my youth and the feelings of rejection I suffered as a result and then the loss of loved ones. These and many more memories fill my mind as though a flood of yesterday could be poured into my today.

Do you realize how many memories I've skipped (good and bad, happy and hurtful)? Hundreds, possibly thousands or tens of thousands of memories that can be recounted, not to mention those that have taken up their abode in my subconscious with the potential of arising without notice.

> **With all the good times ... , I was haunted by this one painful memory!**

Memory is a powerful thing, and in overcoming grief, you will have to deal with memories. Try as you might to forget them, know that they are imbedded deep within the recesses of your mind, never to be lost or actually forgotten. The key is not trying *not* to think about them. Rather, it is how you process them. Let's talk about that for a moment.

I recently had a battle with a painful memory concerning the loss of my son, Bubba. I am not sure what triggered the memory, but it came in like a tidal wave. As much as I tried to put aside the memory, it just kept coming and, with each occurrence, the pain intensified. Much to our chagrin, some memories bring torment. With all the good times we had in our lives, it seems that I was being haunted by this one painful memory.

I had to process this memory in order to put it into proper perspective. I had to remind myself that I had loved Bubba dearly at all times. I had to recall that I asked for forgiveness for ignorantly having caused him pain, and I received that forgiveness.

I reminded myself of how proud I was of Bubba when I asked him to forgive me for not being a better dad (in my eyes), and his response to me brought tears to my eyes and a wellspring of joy and happiness that my son had become a man somewhere in the course of all this.

Finally, after constant bombardment by this one memory, I was able to overcome it as I thought it through. What I have learned through this I want to share with you:

1. You cannot stop memories. No one would purposely bring up painful memories just for the sake of it.

2. Just as pleasant memories will come, painful memories will also arise. Be prepared for them, because they will show up. The occurrence of these may be for the purpose of healing some area in your life that needs to be settled.

3. Process these memories. That is, don't neglect them nor attempt to discard them, but face them head on, knowing that they may well occur again. Hopefully, the next time you will have thought the matter through.

4. Learn how to forgive yourself. Often, we're harder on ourselves than others are. Whether you have offended someone purposely or ignorantly, forgive yourself. It's amazing what age and maturity can produce in us.

5. Purposely remember the good and the positive outcome of each unpleasant memory (and they are there), and then move on within this new light. Do not be afraid to think things through.

You will be amazed how the pain you've just experienced, whether for a day or a prolonged period of time, just disappears, and life goes on with a new and better perspective.

Dealing with Memories

Please note that you may or may not experience this same memory again. If you do, you will be more equipped to quickly handle things with the realization that healing is available through the process.

I'm not necessarily a "country music buff," although I enjoy listening to some good old country music every now and then. It seems to me that over the past ten years or so the trend in country music has changed from "tears in my beer" to actual real-life events. This brings a certain touch to the heart and the music becomes more personal than before. I enjoy that.

One particular artist, Alan Jackson, and a song he sang, "Remember When," really tells the story of life's ups and downs. It speaks to the faculty of remembering. In fact, it touches the good and the difficult and the power of rising above those hard places in life. Some of the lyrics of this song (in no particular order) go like this:

Remember when I was young and so were you
And time stood still and love was all we knew
You were the first, so was I

We made love and then you cried
Remember when?

Remember when old ones died and new were born
And life was changed, disassembled, rearranged
We came together, fell apart
And broke each other's hearts
Remember when?

Remember when the sound of little feet
Was the music we danced to week to week
Brought back the love, we found trust
Vowed we'd never give it up
Remember when? [3]

I am so proud of all my children, not because of what they do or don't do!

---

3. Songwriter: Alan Jackson. "Remember When" lyrics © Sony/ATV Music Publishing LLC

Dealing with Memories

Another artist, Louisiana's own Trace Atkins, sang a song entitled "You're Gonna Miss This." I can relate to this song because I have a daughter that loves me and wants to make me so proud of her who she goes out of her way to please me. Of course she doesn't have to do anything to make me proud of her. I am so proud of all my children, not because of what they do or don't do. Nor because of any of their accomplishments, but because of who they are and that they're mine, and I love them.

Again, the lyrics (in no particular order) go like this:

She was staring out the window of that SUV
Complaining, saying "I can't wait to turn eighteen"
She said "I'll make my own money, and I'll make my own rules"
Momma put the car in park out there in front of the school
She kissed her head and said "I was just like you"

You're gonna miss this
You're gonna want this back
You're gonna wish these days hadn't gone by so fast

These are some good times
So take a good look around
You may not know it now
But you're gonna miss this
Before she knows it she's a brand new bride
In her one-bedroom apartment, and her daddy stops by
He tells her "It's a nice place"
She says "It'll do for now"
Starts talking about babies and buying a house
Daddy shakes his head and says "Baby, just slow down"[4]

Another artist, again a Louisiana boy named Tim McGraw, sang a song entitled "Live Like You Were Dyin." The song speaks of a young man in his early forties who discovered he had cancer, and the lyrics say:

He said
"I was in my early forties
With a lot of life before me
And a moment came that stopped me on a dime
I spent most of the next days

4. Songwriters: Ashley Gorley/Lee Miller. "You're Gonna Miss This" lyrics © Warner Chappell Music, Inc, Spirit Music Group, BMG Rights Management

Dealing with Memories

Looking at the x-rays
Talkin' 'bout the options
And talkin' 'bout sweet time"

I asked him
"When it sank in
That this might really be the real end
How's it hit you
When you get that kind of news?
Man, what'd you do?"

He said
"I went skydiving
I went Rocky Mountain climbing
I went 2.7 seconds on a bull named Fumanchu
And I loved deeper
And I spoke sweeter
And I gave forgiveness I'd been denying"
And he said
"Someday I hope you get the chance
To live like you were dying" [5]

5. Songwriters: Craig Michael Wiseman / James Timothy
   Nichols / Tim Nichols. "Live Like You Were Dying" lyrics
   © Warner Chappell Music, Inc, Round Hill Music Big
   Loud Songs, BMG Rights Management

One final song, this one entitled "Life Ain't Always Beautiful," sung by Gary Allan, has lyrics that are so true to life's paths. In no particular order, the lyrics say:

Life ain't always beautiful
Sometimes it's just plain hard
Life can knock you down
It can break your heart.
Life ain't always beautiful
You think you're on your way
And it's just a dead end road
At the end of the day.

But the struggles make you stronger
And the changes make you wise
And happiness has it's own way
Of taking it's own sweet time.

No, life ain't always beautiful
Tears will fall sometimes
Life ain't always beautiful
But it's a beautiful ride. [6]

6. Songwriters: Tommy Lee James / Cynthia Evelyn Thomson. "Life Ain't Always Beautiful" lyrics © Sony/ATV Music Publishing LLC, BMG Rights Management

Dealing with Memories

These four songs, sung by four great artists, touch the very core of human existence. First, Alan Jackson's "Remember When." How many times has a conversation started with those two words, "remember when?" and memories of days gone by are triggered.

> **These four songs ...**
> **touch the very core of**
> **human existence!**

Remember when you were young and ... ? Remember when you got in trouble in school and ... ? Remember when we went to the beach and ... ? These memories could be pleasant memories, and yet, because of some current void in our lives, they could also bring us pain. We must always remember that pleasant memories are exactly that—pleasant memories—and not allow ourselves to fall victim to despondency due to the absence of a loved one.

Trace Adkins "You're Gonna Miss This" reaches into the deepest recesses of our being. I remember telling my children, "Slow down. You'll grow old soon enough." I didn't want them to miss out on their childhood. I feel, to some degree, that I missed out on so much because of having to grow up too quickly. I don't blame anyone for that. My parents did the best they could in their day, but in that day children worked.

Children want to grow up. Slow them down; they're going to miss this!

Now, there's nothing wrong with children working. In fact, I believe a certain amount of work is vital to a healthy growing up. But I cut my first yard for money when I was six years old. Our age has produced a sickness that we put upon our children in that we expect them to grow up too fast, with young children competing professionally at such young ages in beauty contests, athletics and so many other activities. Children want to grow up fast, but we need to slow them down or they're going to miss too much.

Dealing with Memories

Oh how I miss the days when my children were small. Those were such wonderful days. I cannot allow those good memories to bring sadness to my heart because they're gone. I must live for today and tomorrow.

Tim McGraw's song, "Live Like You Were Dyin," is the sad reality that death hits the young as well as the elderly. It should teach us to live every day as if it is our last on earth. With all of our responsibilities as adults, our occupations and families to raise, let's not forget to achieve our dreams.

Sure, we may not have the means to do everything we want to do, but we can do some of those things. Skydiving may not be one of my pleasures and, for that matter, neither is riding Fumanchu, but loving others and forgiving is relatively inexpensive and these can be done daily.

Instead of laboring on the thought, "I should have reached out earlier," be grateful for when you did reach out and enjoy that memory, allowing it to bring healing to your psyche.

Gary Allan's song, "Life Ain't Always Beautiful," speaks of the issues of life we face, often on a daily basis. My lovely wife Monique loves this song but cannot speak of it without breaking into tears. You see, the truth is that life isn't always filled with pleasurable things. There are disturbing truths about life, but it's the journey that counts. Life may not always be beautiful, but life isn't always ugly either! Always remember, life's a beautiful ride. You will surely gain much comfort from remembering this.

I would be remiss if I didn't include a song of hope that reminds us that when we put our trust in God, all ends well.

The Gaithers sing a beautiful song, "Because He Lives." It is a song that speaks of the ultimate truth of putting our faith in God and His love for us. The lyrics of this timely song go like this:

God sent His son, they called Him Jesus
He came to love, heal and forgive
He lived and died to buy my pardon
An empty grave is there to prove my savior lives

Because He lives, I can face tomorrow
Because He lives, all fear is gone
Because I know He holds the future

Dealing with Memories

And life is worth the living, just because He lives

How sweet to hold a newborn baby
And feel the pride and joy He gives
But greater still the calm assurance
This child can face uncertain day, because He lives

Because He lives, I can face tomorrow
Because He lives, all fear is gone
Because I know He holds the future
And life is worth the living, just because He lives [7]

This song has brought comfort to millions of lives since its first release. Because He lives I can face tomorrow. Allow these words to comfort your heart. I CAN face tomorrow! I WILL make it! I AM healed and I CAN overcome grief! Why? Because One greater than you and I lives in us and is our Enabler to conquer what has been at-

[7] Songwriters: Chris Tomlin/Daniel Carson/Ed Cash/ Gloria Gaither/Jason Ingram/Matt Maher/William J. Gaither. "Because He Lives" lyrics © Warner Chappell Music, Inc, BMG Rights Management, Essential Music Publishing, Capitol Christian Music Group, Music Services, Inc.

tempting to conquer us—grief. Finally, LIFE is worth living! Don't ever give up on living!

> **I WILL make it!**
> **I AM healed**
> **and I CAN overcome grief!**

Amazingly, God has creatively released in us avenues of healing from all of our hurts. From songs to seasons, people to pets, friends to fun, and so many more avenues to assist us in overcoming our pain. Allow me to say that memories are some of the greatest healing channels that we can utilize. Remember that memories are the only things you can take into your future from your past. They will never leave you. Therefore, make good memories every day. Then, when you're lonely or you feel down, draw on the reserve of your memories.

Remember When, You're Gonna Miss This, Live Like You Were Dyin, Life Ain't Always Beautiful and, above all, Because He Lives, I Can Face Tomorrow!

Dealing with Memories

Let me share a Scripture with you as we close this important chapter.

> *To enjoy your work and to accept your lot in life—that is indeed a gift from God. The person who does that will not need to look back with sorrow on his past, for God gives him joy.* Ecclesiastes 5:20, TLB

03 10 80

PRESSING THROUGH YOUR PAIN

"But it hurts so much. How long will this hurt go on?" How many times have I heard a grieving person say that? How many times have I said it? I'm sure it's more than I care to remember. But it's the truth. It does hurt so much. It's almost an unbearable pain that debilitates and nearly cripples us beyond repair. All your strength and energy have been emptied from you, and you're weakened and seemingly without hope.

How do I overcome the pain? How do I get over this? Will I ever get over this? Let me say to you, YES! And let that yes echo in your heart. You will get over this! I will get over this! My purpose in this chapter is to assist you in pressing through, pressing through the pain to healing.

I believe that once the initial shock of losing a loved one is realized, healing begins. You've accepted the sad fact that a loved one is gone and will never return again. Let me speak to this point for a moment.

I believe in a place called Heaven. I understand, from studying the Word of God, that this is a place that God Himself has prepared for us. I also understand that Heaven is off-limits to death, sickness, sadness, loneliness, pain and all other things that disturb our living. All of these comprise a short list of interruptions that take occasion in our lives. Heaven is void of them all.

One way I've learned to move through a season of grief is to know that I will eventually be reunited with my dearly departed, never to be separated again! There is comfort in knowing that death doesn't win; we do! Death may have knocked you down, but it hasn't knocked you out! Death may have taken the wind out of you for a moment, but there's a fresh breath coming to you that will revive in you a greater hope than ever before.

An old hymn of the church says it like this:

There'll be no sorrows there,
No more burdens to bear,
No more sickness, no pain,
No more parting over there.
And forever I will be
With the One who died for me.
What a day, glorious day that will be! [8]

I'm telling you that death is not final! There are better days ahead of you, as well as the ultimate day when we are all reunited with our loved ones in that place called Heaven.

My purpose is to assist you in pressing through the pain to healing!

Pressing through is, at times, a daily, weekly, monthly or even longer encounter, while, at other

---

8. Songwriter: Jim Hill. "What A Day That Will Be" lyrics © Ben Speer Music

times, it may be moment to moment. It appears to me that we may never forget how much we've hurt over the death of a loved one, but there comes a time when we will no longer experience pain or even be threatened by the pain of their departure.

You'll have to do what you don't feel like doing!

Time is in our favor when it comes to overcoming grief ... if it hasn't been dragged out too long. Believe me, I know! It will get better with time. But in order for it to get better, you must "press through." By "pressing through" I mean that you must make a conscious effort to overcome grief. It means that you will have to be stronger than the hopelessness you may be experiencing. It means that you'll have to do what you don't feel like doing—getting involved, staying busy doing something that will remove your mind from hurt, to enable healing.

I've have often heard it said in the church, "You're going to have to have a made-up mind!" That is a saying applicable to this subject. You must make up your mind that this loss will not destroy you. You must refuse to allow grief to get an advantage over you and dominate your life. Make up your mind that life is worth living, that there are other loved ones who need you and depend upon you. Make up your mind that this thing will not do you in. You are stronger than death, and you will overcome it. Do you have a made-up mind?

Something else I've seen that can be helpful is this: when I find myself being attacked with thoughts that will lead to emotional pain, if I will involve myself in doing something that I enjoy doing, it replaces my energy and removes the thoughts I was about to experience. For example, I enjoy speaking with friends and family and just love being around people in general. When I am faced with painful memories, if I can surround myself with loved ones, the memories subside, and I feel so much better. Therefore, I purposely attempt to involve myself in things that I enjoy doing, so that I can get over certain memories.

Now, let me say to you that this is a temporary fix. The memories will return, but when they do, I will have had time to gather my thoughts, gain strength and prepare to face such memories, in order that I may be healed. It becomes easier to deal with such memories when I know that I am properly prepared for their return.

> **Make up your mind that this loss will not destroy you!**

Another way of pressing through involves our thought patterns. I affirm that you can consciously develop thought patterns that enable you to overcome grief. Your thoughts dominate your life and are inroads to your decision making. What do you think about most of the time? Find out what it is, examine it closely and see if these thoughts have not forged a lifestyle within you. Your thoughts will ultimately determine your actions.

The Bible has a lot to say about our thoughts, but I'd like to present to you one powerful scripture that has helped many to overcome their bad experiences. Paul, writing to the church at Philippi, said this:

> *Finally, brethren, whatsoever things are true, whatsoever things are honest, whatsoever things are just, whatsoever things are pure, whatsoever things are lovely, whatsoever things are of good report; if there be any virtue, and if there be any praise, THINK ON THESE THINGS.* Philippians 4:8
> (Emphasis Mine)

If you can fill your mind with these kinds of thoughts, rest assured that you are on your way to total healing over grief. Press through, because you're going to make it!

❧ **11** ❧

My Closing Remarks

I realize that this has been a difficult subject to address. In fact, for some, it may have aroused some of those emotions we wrote of. But, not to fret, you will be normal again. Praise God!

I want to say that it is imperative that you have a pastor in your life. I say this, not only because I am a pastor, but because I've needed a pastor as I went through my experiences of losing loved ones.

I am eternally grateful for the pastors who surrounded me during my times of grief. My pastor and dear friend, Irvin McCorkle, drove more than eight hours just to be with me when my son passed away. He said very little, but what he did say was what I needed to hear, and what he didn't say spoke volumes to me too.

An evangelist and a very close friend of mine, Rev. Jachin Dardar, put on a "pastors hat" and performed the funeral ceremony. Again, because of my relationship with him for more than forty years, I had a pastor to lean upon. He said the right things, inspired by God, and he didn't say what is 'normally' said at funerals. The understanding these men possessed assisted in my healing and my ability to move beyond the most difficult time of my life and move on.

> **It is imperative that you have a pastor in your life!**

If you don't have a pastor, one who shepherds you, invests time in you and imparts vision and God's Word into you, find one! I'm not talking about a preacher or a minister who has an ulterior motive, but one who has been kissed by God to love and nurture others in all seasons of their lives.

My Closing Remarks

I have performed far too many funerals for those whose loved ones had no pastor. The saddest funeral I ever did was not of a baby who passed away without reason. Nor was it of a father who died and left behind a wife and children. No, it was the funeral of a young man who died tragically in an automobile accident, and no minister in the entire area would perform the ceremony. Now, that was sad! Everybody needs a pastor!

Everybody needs someone in their lives to share intimately what cannot be shared openly. For me, it is my wife, Monique, to whom I am indebted as she stood with me through the tragic loss of my son. She made no pretence of understanding what, why, or how. She just stood with me.

Monique allowed me to weep when I needed to weep. She wept with me when I needed someone to weep with, but she also understood when I needed to weep alone. She listened to countless hours of my reminiscing about the life I'd had with my son. The most important thing of all was that she was there. She was a God-send to help me heal. Her words were always filled with grace, and love and her support for me—both spiritually and emotionally—were beyond words.

> # Everybody needs a friend or a group of friends!

Everybody needs a friend or a group of friends to speak with. I'm not speaking of a community support group; I'm talking about true friends. A true friend is someone who will listen to you when you need it and speak with you when you need it. True friends can range from close associates to family members.

A true friend will not be bothered if you call them at two or three in the morning just to "talk." A true friend will call you to check on you during your mourning process. A true friend will pray for and with you. A true friend will be there "at the drop of a hat" if need be.

My Closing Remarks

Everybody needs to prepare in advance (as much as possible) for the inevitability of death. Talk openly with your loved ones about your desires and keep things in order. Personally, I want to see to it that there are as few loose ends as possible for others to gather up following my departure.

> **Everybody needs to prepare in advance!**

Some may ask, "How is that possible when you're not sure when you will have to face death or which one of you will go first?" The most important thing is to know that you are right with God. Having God in your life makes all the difference. And, since Jesus is the One who conquered death, Hell and the grave, having Him on your side will ensure that you have the best in this life and also in the life to come.

Too often we hear about eternity only at funerals. This is a subject we all need to address more often. We need more pastors who tell the truth about the inevitability of death and help us to get ready for eternity. God's Word is rich in truths that will enable you to prepare for death and carry on when others pass on before you. The Word of God can impart to you the wisdom, love, direction and comfort of an all-wise God. His Word is life.

Death devastates lives, disintegrates futures and defies human reasoning. God and His Word establish life, secure futures and go beyond human reasoning. A firm relationship with God and His Word cannot be easily shaken through tragedy—any tragedy. When you fully trust God for all things, you may be hurt and temporarily devastated, but you can have full confidence that in time everything will all right again!

You may think that I'm saying this because I'm a pastor. Yes, I am a pastor, but that's not why I'm saying this. You see, I am also a husband, a father, a brother and a friend who's been touched by death and have overcome its sting.

Apart from God, there is no one who will walk with you through the entirety of the healing process. Be grateful for family and friends and others who assist you during your periods of grief. But let me say to you that when the lights are turned out at night and you have retired for the evening, God is still there beside you, ministering healing even during the darkest nights of your life. Therefore, everybody needs God!

> **Everybody needs God!**

OUR THANKS

Monique and I are honored to serve as The Baldwin Church in Baldwin, Louisiana. We are equally blessed to minister in other churches in this great nation of ours as well as other countries. With a Pastor/Evangelist mantle, we focus our attention on the message God has for His people and deliver it with integrity. We are in the beginning stages of the greatest move of Cod to this point in history. Get ready for a great ride!

I want to declare it without hesitation: We are in the season of the Lord! Regardless of how things may appear, His Word does not change, nor will my declarations.

Our Thanks

Monique and I want to express our appreciation for your investment in this book. This writing is one of hope, one of victory. One way we conquer the "sting" of death is by not allowing it to rule over us when we have lost a loved one. I want you to know that it *does* get better, and it *will* get better. Healing is not only *possible*; if you make the decision to be healed, it is *inevitable*. We shall overcome.

I've been told that a writing of this nature is well overdue. I understand why there is so little written about the subject. It brings back memories—good ones and the not so good. But it also reveals the areas of healing already achieved and those areas still needing complete healing.

For the past forty-six years of dealing with the emotions associated with losing loved ones (mine and multiple hundreds of others), I felt moved by God to release the understandings I have received as well as the path to healing.

Again, we want to thank you for purchasing this book. Your purchase assists us in releasing other writings to help the Body of Christ. Check out our web-site, to remain current with our travels, and please pray with us.

If you've lost a loved one or a friend and would like for us to pray with you, drop us a note by e-mail or letter, and we'll be more than willing to minister to you. Also, if we're ever in your area to minister, please come and see us. We'd love to meet you.

Whole Again!

Jerry & Monique

Author Contact Page

On the Web:
http://jerryfitchministries.com/

E-mail:
decajun2@aol.com

Phone:
(337) 831-0536

Mail:
Jerry and Monique Fitch
4204 Eldridge Street
New Iberia, LA 70563

BOOKS BY JERRY FITCH

Seasons of Suddenlies

...and other revelations of God's times and seasons

by Dr. Jerry Fitch

Introduction by Dr. Jerry Edmon

Moving

through

a Season
of Grief

You have turned my mourning into joyful dancing.
You have taken away my clothes of mourning and clothed me with joy.
Psalm 30:11

Jerry Fitch

THE
FINAL
CALL
ARE WE PRESENTLY RECEIVING THE FINAL CALL OF THE SPIRIT?
JERRY FITCH

COMMUNION

TRUTH
VS.
TRADITION

JERRY FITCH